Elements

by Lynn Van Gorp

Science Contributor
Sally Ride Science
Science Consultants
Michael E. Kopecky, Science Educator
Jane Weir, Physicist

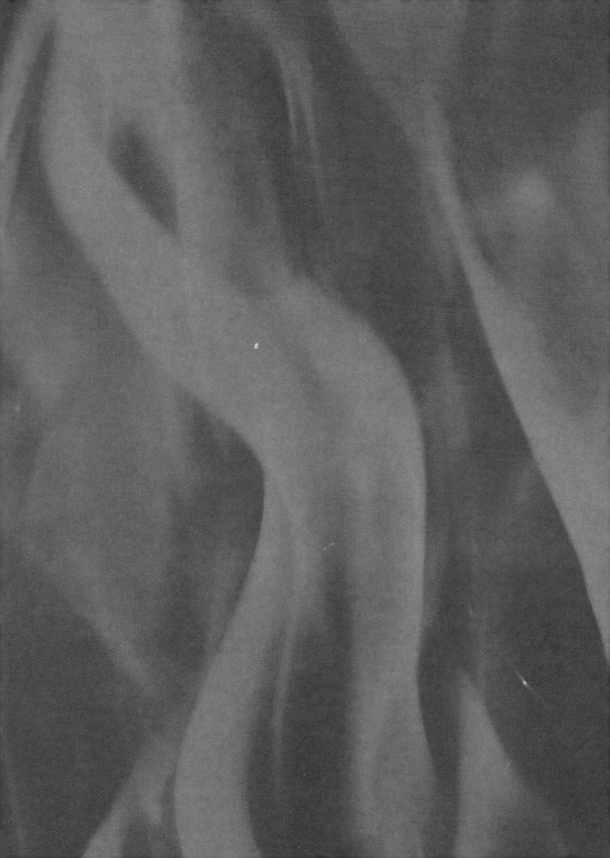

First hardcover edition published in 2009 by
Compass Point Books
151 Good Counsel Drive
P.O. Box 669
Mankato, MN 56002-0669

Editor: Robert McConnell
Designer: Heidi Thompson

Art Director: LuAnn Ascheman-Adams
Creative Director: Keith Griffin
Editorial Director: Nick Healy
Managing Editor: Catherine Neitge

 This book was manufactured with paper containing at least 10 percent post-consumer waste.

Library of Congress Cataloging-in-Publication Data
Van Gorp, Lynn.
  Elements / by Lynn Van Gorp.
    p. cm.—(Mission: Science)
  Includes index.
  ISBN 978-0-7565-3951-1 (library binding)
  1. Matter—Constitution—Juvenile literature. I. Title. II. Series.
  QC173.16.V36 2008
  540—dc22   2008007284

Visit Compass Point Books on the Internet at *www.compasspointbooks.com*
or e-mail your request to *custserv@compasspointbooks.com*

Table of Contents

Matter Is Everywhere

You and this book have something important in common. You might not think you are like the book at all. After all, you are a living thing, and the book is not. But you and the book are both made of matter.

Matter makes up everything in the universe. Big or small, light or heavy, strong or weak, solid or liquid, or even gas—it makes no difference. All of it is matter. Matter is everywhere within you and everywhere around you.

All matter can be detected and measured. The senses help us detect matter. We can see, feel, and smell some matter. For example, we can see a tree, touch its bark, and smell its flowers. But some matter is too small to see with the eyes alone. Microscopes are needed. With them, the very small parts that make up matter, atoms, can be seen.

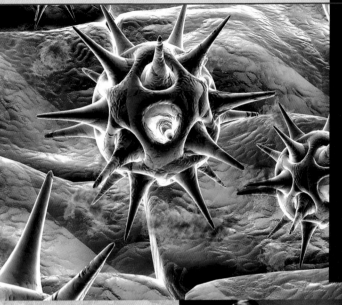

Mega Magnifier

Did you know that an electron microscope can magnify something up to 1 million times its normal size? The microscope uses electrons instead of light to create images of very small things. An electron is a tiny part of an atom.

Micro-organisms scanned by an electron microscope

The scanning electron microscope scans a sample with a beam of electrons. The beam may be scattered off the sample, or it may cause electrons to be emitted by it. These electrons are collected and shown as a 3-D image.

What Are Elements?

An atom is the smallest part of matter. Whatever the matter or its form, it is made of atoms. Think of atoms as being like blocks. You can build just about anything you can imagine with the blocks. Atoms are like that. Combined, atoms can be anything in the universe.

If the atoms that make up something are all the same type, they form an element. An element is a pure substance because it contains only one type of atom. No matter how hard we try, we cannot split an element into anything simpler. Imagine making a stack of red blocks, all the same size. The tower of blocks is like an element. All the pieces are the same. If atoms were blocks, then molecules would be blocks that are put together. If a combination is made of the same type of atoms, or blocks, the molecule is an element. If the atoms are different, it is still a molecule, but it's not an element.

There are 94 elements that occur naturally, which means they can be found in nature. Others are man-made. Oxygen is a natural element that you know well, because you breathe it.

The air we breathe is made of many gases, including oxygen. Oxygen is an element.

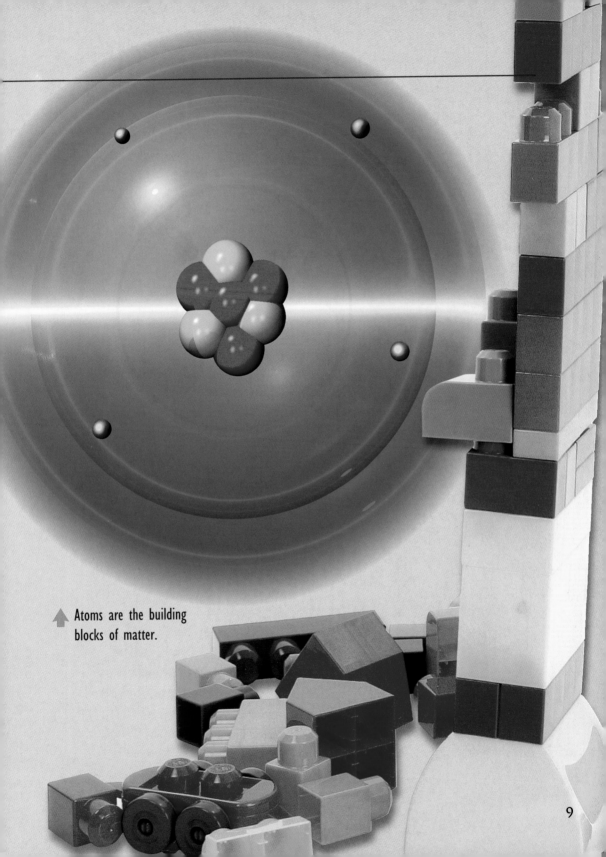

Atoms are the building blocks of matter.

9

Antoine Lavoisier (1743—1794)

Antoine Laurent Lavoisier, a French chemist in the 1700s, gave oxygen its name. He also proved that water is made of oxygen and hydrogen. Lavoisier is known as the founder of modern chemistry.

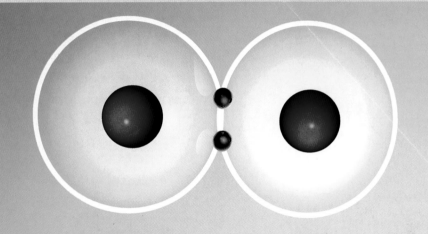

Hydrogen atom + Hydrogen atom = Hydrogen molecule

A molecule is formed when two or more atoms combine. The simplest molecule contains two of the same atoms. An example is the hydrogen molecule, which is simply made of two hydrogen atoms. Most molecules contain two or more different atoms from different elements. Water is probably the best-known molecule. It contains two hydrogen atoms and one oxygen atom. Because it contains different types of atoms, water is not an element.

H_2O

Have you ever heard people ask for "H_2O"? They are asking for water. Its two hydrogen molecules are written as H_2. Its one oxygen molecule is written as O. Together they are written as H_2O.

Water molecule

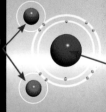

Hydrogen atoms

Oxygen atom

Making Compounds

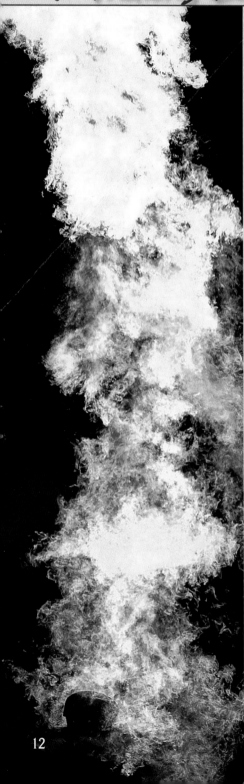

Two or more elements can combine to form a compound. Compounds are different from the elements that make them. Compounds have their own properties, which means they behave in their own ways.

Take the example of water. Water is made of two hydrogen atoms and one oxygen atom. As long as these atoms stay together, they are water molecules. If they separate, they become two gases: hydrogen and oxygen. Water, hydrogen, and oxygen all have different properties. For example, water cannot catch fire, but hydrogen and oxygen can.

◀ Oxygen burning

▲ Chlorine gas

+

A Common Compound

The compound sodium chloride is added to many of the foods we eat. Do you like salty foods, such as french fries? That salty taste is sodium chloride, which is table salt. Sodium is a solid that reacts explosively with water. Chlorine is a green, poisonous gas. Combine them, and they become salt. Salt isn't green, explosive, or poisonous. That is because compounds don't have the properties of the elements that combined to make them.

Sodium = Salt

Chemical Bonds

To understand how compounds are made, you need to know a little more about atoms. Atoms are made of protons, neutrons, and electrons. The protons and neutrons make up the nucleus of an atom. The nucleus is the atom's tightly packed center. Electrons whirl around the nucleus like tiny satellites.

Protons and electrons have opposite electric charges. Protons have positive charges (think of a plus sign in math), and electrons have negative charges (a minus sign). Neutrons are electrically neutral—meaning that they have no charge.

An atom tries to have the same number of protons and electrons (pluses and minuses). This keeps the atom electrically balanced. When atoms have too many electrons or not enough, they do something about it. They either give up their electrons or share them with other atoms.

Remember, compounds are made of two or more elements. The elements need a force to hold them together. That force is called a chemical bond. Chemical bonds are formed when atoms give up or share electrons.

Did You Know?

It is much harder to separate the atoms in naturally occurring molecules than it is to keep them combined. To separate the hydrogen and oxygen atoms that make up water, an electric current or heat is needed.

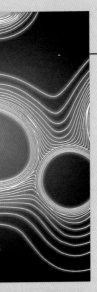
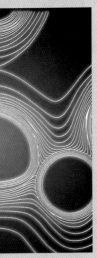

Atoms are drawn to one another because they don't have enough electrons on their own. Atoms try to have an equal number of protons and electrons.

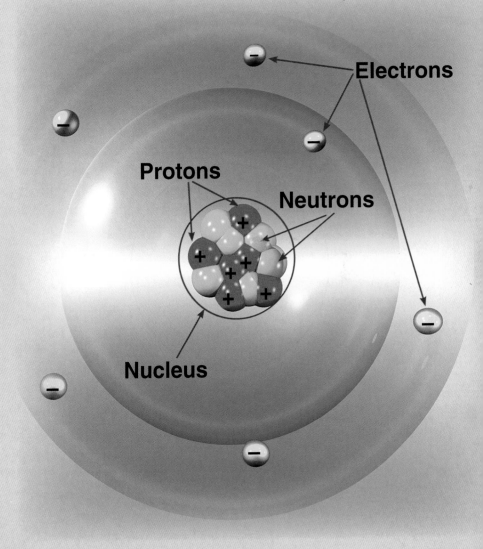

Electrons

Protons

Neutrons

Nucleus

Ionic Bonds

There are two types of chemical bonds: ionic bonds and covalent bonds. These bonds form two types of compounds.

Ionic bonds are bonds created when one or more electrons from one atom are transferred to another atom. The atom that loses electrons is no longer electrically balanced. It has a positive charge. The atom that gains electrons has a negative charge. The opposite charges attract each other. So the atoms form an ionic bond. Ionic bonds are the glue that creates ionic compounds.

Salt is an example of the ionic bonding of the elements sodium and chlorine. As the diagram shows, a sodium atom gives up one of its electrons to a chlorine atom. This creates an electrical attraction, which is an ionic bond. So salt is an ionic compound.

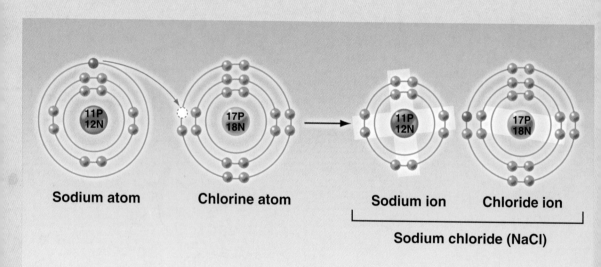

Sodium atom   Chlorine atom   Sodium ion   Chloride ion

Sodium chloride (NaCl)

NaCl is also known as salt. The Wieliczka Salt Mine in Poland is home to beautiful figures that are carved from salt. Just think of all the chemical bonds that are in this much NaCl!

Atoms, Plus and Minus

An ion is an atom with an electric charge. If the charge is positive, it is a positive ion. If the charge is negative, it is a negative ion.

Na

Na

(−) electron

(+) ion

Covalent Bonds

The other type of chemical bonds, covalent bonds, are bonds created when atoms share one or more electrons. The shared electrons spend time between each of the two atoms. The electrons are negatively charged, so they attract the positive nuclei of the two atoms.

(*Nuclei* means more than one nucleus.) Covalent bonds create covalent compounds.

Water is an example of a covalent compound. As you can see in the diagram, each of the two hydrogen atoms shares electrons with the oxygen atom.

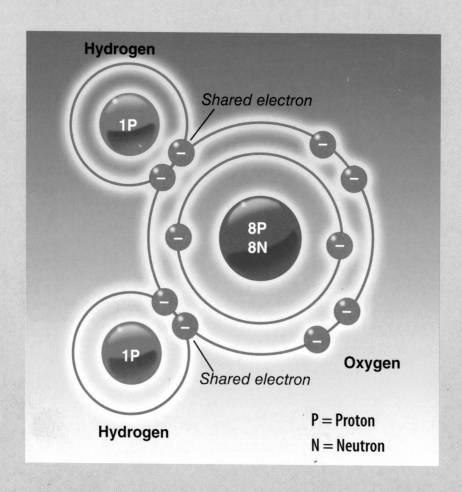

Hydrogen

1P

Shared electron

8P
8N

1P

Shared electron

Oxygen

Hydrogen

P = Proton

N = Neutron

Early Chemist

Long before women were allowed into labs and schools to study science, some women were doing all they could to study it anyway. One such woman was Marie Meurdrac, in France. In 1666, she published the book *Charitable and Easy Chemistry for Women*.

She had learned a lot about medicines. Some of what she learned was used to help the poor. That is what she meant by "charitable" in the title. She thought her knowledge could help people to help others in turn.

Not only did the book include information about medicine, but it also had a section about makeup. It gave important warnings about common makeup ingredients, such as lead, that were poisonous. Her book was popular for many years and was translated into German and Italian.

Did You Know?

During the Restoration era, when Marie Meurdrac lived in France, men and women used cosmetics made of lead—which is poisonous!

Organizing the Elements

Dimitri Mendeleev, a chemist from Siberia, was the youngest of 14 children. When his father died, his mother put all of her energy into getting Dmitri a good education. He loved science, so she helped him follow that dream.

▲ Dimitri Mendeleev (1834–1907)

Mendeleev studied chemistry. He learned about the elements, but he thought they should be organized. In 1869, he decided to organize all the known elements into a chart. This chart, called the Periodic Table of the Elements, has a lot more elements today, but it is still a basic tool used by scientists.

In the table, elements are arranged in rows and columns. They are placed according to their atomic number. An element's atomic number is the number of protons in one atom of the element. The elements are shown by using chemical symbols, which are short forms of the elements' names.

Each row of elements is called a period. Each column of the table is called a group or family. Elements in the same area of the table usually have similar properties.

In the periodic table, elements are listed by their chemical symbols. Chemists refer to the elements by using these symbols.

Symbol	Element
Fe	Iron
Au	Gold
He	Helium
N	Nitrogen

ПЕРИОДИЧЕСКАЯ СИСТЕМА ЭЛЕМЕНТОВ

Mendeleev's Periodic Table of the Elements

When Mendeleev's table was created, there were 70 known elements. He believed there were more than 70 and that the unknown elements could be predicted. He left spaces in his table for elements that hadn't yet been discovered. He believed that elements would be found to fill those gaps. During his life, three of the elements he predicted were discovered.

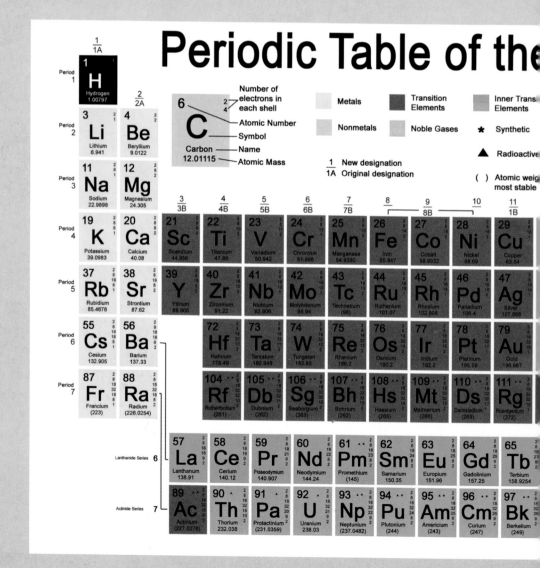

Periodic Table of the

Did You Know?

About one-fourth of all the known elements have been added to the periodic table since 1923.

Reading the Table

The basic information in each box in the table is the element's name, chemical symbol, and atomic number. For example, the chemical symbol for iron is Fe. Its atomic number is 26. A number at the bottom is its atomic mass. Mass means the amount of matter that is in one atom of the element.

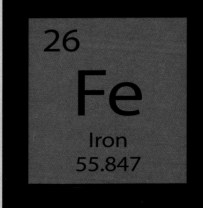

26	
	Fe
	Iron
	55.847

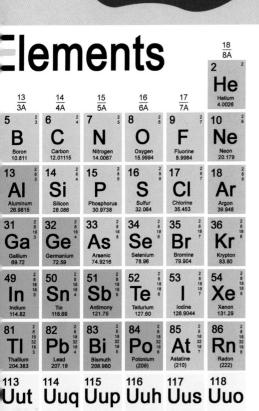

Elements

					18 8A
					2 2 **He** Helium 4.0026

13 3A	14 4A	15 5A	16 6A	17 7A	
5 2 3 **B** Boron 10.811	6 2 4 **C** Carbon 12.01115	7 2 5 **N** Nitrogen 14.0067	8 2 6 **O** Oxygen 15.9994	9 2 7 **F** Fluorine 8.9984	10 2 8 **Ne** Neon 20.179
13 2 8 3 **Al** Aluminum 26.9815	14 2 8 4 **Si** Silicon 28.086	15 2 8 5 **P** Phosphorus 30.9738	16 2 8 6 **S** Sulfur 32.064	17 2 8 5 **Cl** Chlorine 35.453	18 2 8 8 **Ar** Argon 39.948
31 2 8 18 3 **Ga** Gallium 69.72	32 2 8 18 4 **Ge** Germanium 72.59	33 2 8 18 5 **As** Arsenic 74.9216	34 2 8 18 6 **Se** Selenium 78.96	35 2 8 18 7 **Br** Bromine 79.904	36 2 8 18 8 **Kr** Krypton 83.80
49 2 8 18 3 **In** Indium 114.82	50 2 8 18 4 **Sn** Tin 118.69	51 2 8 18 5 **Sb** Antimony 121.75	52 2 8 18 6 **Te** Tellurium 127.60	53 2 8 18 7 **I** Iodine 126.9044	54 2 8 18 8 **Xe** Xenon 131.29
81 2 8 18 32 3 **Tl** Thallium 204.383	82 2 8 18 32 4 **Pb** Lead 207.19	83 2 8 18 32 5 **Bi** Bismuth 208.980	84 2 8 18 32 6 **Po** Polonium (209)	85 2 8 18 32 7 **At** Astatine (210)	86 2 8 18 32 8 **Rn** Radon (222)
113 **Uut**	114 **Uuq**	115 **Uup**	116 **Uuh**	117 **Uus**	118 **Uuo**

Unknown elements 113 - 118 are shown in their predicted positions.

67 2 8 18 29 8 2 **Ho** Holmium 164.930	68 2 8 18 30 8 2 **Er** Erbium 167.26	69 2 8 18 31 8 2 **Tm** Thulium 168.934	70 2 8 18 32 8 2 **Yb** Ytterbium 173.04	71 2 8 18 32 9 2 **Lu** Lutetium 174.97
99 ·· 2 8 18 18 8 2 **Es** Einsteinium (252)	100 ·· 2 8 18 18 8 2 **Fm** Fermium (257)	101 ·· 2 8 18 31 8 2 **Md** Mendelevium (258)	102 ·· 2 8 18 32 8 2 **No** Nobelium (259)	103 ·· 2 8 18 32 9 2 **Lr** Lawrencium (260)

Some scientists spend their careers studying the periodic table and the elements. You might see a modern periodic table hanging on a classroom wall.

Chemical Symbols and Formulas

Scientists use symbols because it is easier and faster than writing out the names of elements, molecules, and compounds. For example, the symbol for the element sodium is Na. The symbol for chlorine is Cl.

The combination of two or more elements to form a molecule is shown by writing their symbols next to each other. That is a chemical formula. The formula for sodium chloride (salt) is NaCl.

If an element has more than one atom in its molecule, the formula uses a small number after its symbol. For example, water is H_2O, which means there are two atoms of hydrogen and one atom of oxygen in the molecule.

To show the number of molecules, a full-sized number is put in front of the molecule symbol. For example, four molecules of carbon dioxide would be written as $4CO_2$.

47
Ag
Silver
107.868

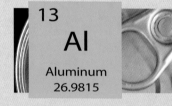

13
Al
Aluminum
26.9815

29
Cu
Copper
63.54

79
Au
Gold
196.967

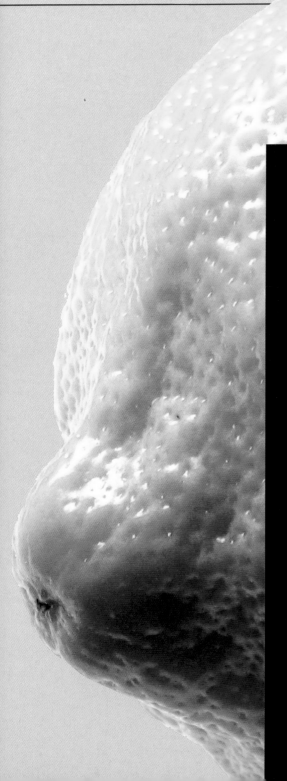

Cool Chemistry

You can use chemistry to write and read invisible messages. First write a message on a sheet of paper using a small paintbrush and lemon juice. Then use one of these two ways to read the message:

1. Hold your paper to a lightbulb or other heat source. (Don't hold it near a flame.) Lemon juice is an acid, and it weakens paper. When the paper is heated, the weakened areas of the paper, where the lemon juice is, will turn brown before the rest of the paper does. Your message will appear.

2. Dip your paper with the lemon-juice message into a diluted iodine solution. That is a mixture of iodine and water. Paper is made of cellulose, which will trap the iodine molecules. That will turn the paper blue. The vitamin C from the lemon juice "ink" will react with iodine to make the message's letters white.

When Chemicals React

In chemistry, a reaction happens when one or more elements change into one or more new substances.

For it to be a reaction, the chemicals must respond to each other, and a chemical change must occur. In other words, something new has to be created.

When iron oxidizes (is exposed to oxygen), rust is produced. The iron chemically combines with the oxygen to produce the rust. This process is called a chemical reaction.

Chemical reactions always create new substances. The new substances are made out of the elements of the original substances.

Iron oxide is created from iron and oxygen. No new elements are made—just a new compound. Iron + oxygen = iron oxide (rust). This can also be written with chemical symbols:

$$Fe + O_2 = FeO_2$$

Iron and oxygen are still present in rust even though what you see looks like neither one.

A Chemical Reaction That You Can Create

You can make raisins dance by putting them in baking soda (sodium bicarbonate) and vinegar.

The baking soda reacts with an acid in the vinegar to form carbon dioxide gas. The gas bubbles stick to the raisins, making the raisins lighter than the water. The bubbles push the raisins up to the surface of the water. When the bubbles and raisins reach the surface, the bubbles burst. This makes the raisins heavier again, so they sink.

This keeps happening as long as the chemical reaction continues. When the bubbles stop forming, the raisins no longer move. Try it!

Mixtures and Solutions

Mixtures are different from chemical compounds. Mixtures do not combine chemically. A mixture can contain elements and molecules in any amount. The items in a mixture can keep their original properties, and they can be returned to their original forms.

For example, sand is a mixture of solids. The individual particles in sand do not change when they mix together. They can be separated easily.

A solution is a mixture that is created when some elements or compounds are combined with others. Many solutions are liquids. They are made when a liquid, solid, or gas dissolves in a liquid. An example is sweetened tea, which is created by dissolving sugar in liquid tea. But some solutions are gases or solids.

When a solution has been created, it has the same properties throughout. Vinegar is a solution of water and acetic acid. The vinegar that we use in food is 5 percent acid and 95 percent water. The water and acid do not separate—they stay together—but there is no chemical reaction.

A glass of tea with sugar is a tasty solution.

An Enormous Mixture ... of Sand

The Sahara Desert, in northern Africa, is larger than 3.6 million square miles (9 million square kilometers). It is the largest desert in the world. Most of it is covered with sand—a giant mixture!

Balls have provided fun for centuries. Early balls were made from stitched-up cloth, animal skulls, and pig or cow bladders. Now balls are products of chemistry.

In this activity, you will combine several compounds to create a bouncy ball. The process of making the ball is a chemical reaction.

Materials

- borax powder
- white glue
- cornstarch
- water
- pen
- two small cups
- measuring spoons
- craft stick
- small plastic bags

Procedure

1   Label one cup "Borax Solution."

2   Put two tablespoons of warm water into the cup.

3   Add one-half teaspoon of borax powder.

4   Stir with the craft stick until the borax is completely dissolved in the water.

5   Label the other cup "Ball Mix."

6 Put one tablespoon of white glue into the Ball Mix cup.

7 Add one-half teaspoon of the Borax Solution to the Ball Mix. Do not mix yet.

8 Add one tablespoon of cornstarch to the Ball Mix. Wait 10 to 15 seconds before mixing.

9 Stir the new Ball Mix until it is no longer possible to stir.

10 Take the mixture out of the cup, and press it and squeeze it. Keep doing this until the mixture holds a ball shape.

Your ball is finished!

Store it in the plastic bag to keep it fresh.

Try Some Variations

Experiment with the amount of each compound you use to make the ball. Change only one compound at a time. Each time you make a change, record the amount of each compound you use and your results.

Glossary

atom—smallest particle of an element

atomic mass—amount of matter in one atom of an element; sometimes called atomic weight

atomic number—number of protons in an element's atom

chemical bond—force that binds atoms together to form molecules

chemical formula—use of symbols to show the names of elements, molecules, and compounds and their relationships

chemical reaction—process in which one or more substances are made into a new substance or substances

chemical symbol—shorthand or chemical abbreviation for an element; Fe is the chemical symbol for iron

compound—substance made of two or more elements that are bonded together

covalent bond—chemical bond in which atoms share one or more electrons

electron—negatively charged particle that whirls around the nucleus of an atom

element—substance that cannot be broken down into simpler substances

ion—electrically charged atom

ionic bond—chemical bond in which an atom has given one or more electrons to another atom

matter—particles of which everything in the universe is made

microscope—device that uses lenses to magnify very small objects for scientific study

mixture—combination of substances that was created without a chemical reaction

molecule—group of two or more atoms that are bonded together

neutron—particle in the nucleus of an atom that has no electric charge

properties—qualities of something

proton—positively charged particle in the nucleus of an atom

solution—mixture created when some elements or compounds are combined with others without a chemical reaction; can be a solid, liquid, or gas

Robert Boyle (1627–1691)
Irish scientist and one of the first modern chemists who was a pioneer in doing careful experimentation and demonstrated that—contrary to some ancient beliefs—air, earth, fire, and water are not elements

Marie Sklodowska Curie (1867–1934)
French scientist and first woman to win a Nobel Prize who did important research on radioactivity and, with her husband, Pierre Curie, discovered two radioactive elements, radium and polonium

John Dalton (1766–1844)
English chemist who believed that each element has only one type of atom and that all of its atoms have the same mass and the same properties

Antoine Lavoisier (1743–1794)
French chemist, known as the founder of modern chemistry, who identified many elements, created a system for naming chemical compounds, discovered the law of conservation of mass, and wrote the first modern chemistry textbook

Dimitri Mendeleev (1834–1907)
Russian chemist who discovered similarities in groups of elements based on their mass and who created the Periodic Table of the Elements, a chart that organized all known elements and (in expanded form) is still a basic tool of science

Linus Pauling (1901–1994)
American chemist who described the nature of the chemical bond, the force that holds atoms together in molecules

Chemistry Through Time

Prehistoric Era	Fire, a chemical reaction, is caused and controlled by people
c. 3500 B.C.	Bronze is made by melting and combining copper and arsenic
c. 400 B.C.	Democritus claims that the atom is the simplest form of matter, is invisible, and cannot be destroyed
400s B.C.	Empedocles says four elements—fire, air, earth, and water—form all other substances
300s B.C.	Aristotle argues that fire, air, earth, or water can be changed into any of the other three elements by changing heat and moisture
c. 1– 1700 A.D.	Alchemists try unsuccessfully to create gold and silver from cheap metals; they also fail to find a substance to cure diseases and let people live longer
1600s	Robert Boyle disproves Aristotle's theory of the four elements; he also finds new ways to identify and analyze substances
Late 1700s	Antoine Lavoisier develops the law of the conservation of matter, identifies oxygen and other substances as elements, and creates a system (still in use) for naming chemical compounds based on the elements in them
1803	John Dalton's atomic theory declares that each element has a particular kind of atom; he also argues that all of an element's atoms have the same mass and properties
1869	Dimitri Mendeleev publishes the first modern Periodic Table of the Elements, which classifies elements according to their atomic masses and properties

1898	Marie Sklodowska Curie and her husband, Pierre, study uranium and thorium and call the spontaneous decay "radioactivity"; they also discover two elements: polonium and radium.
1902	Wilhelm Wien identifies the proton
1911	Ernest Rutherford creates a model of the atom that has a positively charged nucleus surrounded by fast-moving, negatively charged electrons
1916	Gilbert Lewis argues that the bond between a molecule's atoms is created by their sharing of two electrons
1929	John Cockcroft and Ernest Walton invent the first particle accelerator (a machine that propels tiny pieces of matter at high speed) capable of breaking up the nuclei of atoms
1932	James Chadwick discovers the neutron, which is in an atom's nucleus and has no electric charge
1934	Enrico Fermi fires neutrons at elements; he later splits the atom and helps to create the atomic bombs dropped on Japan in 1945 to end World War II
1980s	Scientists start trying to find a way to use the sun's energy to make hydrogen fuel out of water
2000s	Scientists and engineers make many new materials and useful products using nanotechnology, the science of working with objects as tiny as an atom

Cooper, Sharon Katz. *The Periodic Table: Mapping the Elements*. Minneapolis: Compass Point Books, 2007.

Miller, Ron. *The Elements: What You Really Want to Know*. Minneapolis: Twenty-First Century Books, 2006.

Newmark, Ann. *Eyewitness: Chemistry*. New York: DK Children, 2000.

Stille, Darlene. *Chemical Change: From Fireworks to Rust*. Minneapolis: Compass Point Books, 2006.

Whyman, Kathryn. *Everyday Chemicals*. North Mankato, Minn.: Stargazer, 2004.

On the Web

For more information on this topic, use FactHound.

1. Go to *www.facthound.com*

2. Type in this book ID: 075653951X

3. Click on the *Fetch It* button.

FactHound will find the best Web sites for you.

Index

Lynn Van Gorp

Lynn Van Gorp graduated with a master of science degree from the University of Calgary, Canada, and did additional graduate work at the University of Washington, Seattle, and the University of California, Irvine. She has taught for more than 30 years, at the elementary and middle-school levels and at the university level. Her educational focus areas include science, reading, and technology. Lynn has written a number of student- and teacher-based curriculum-related publications.

Image Credits

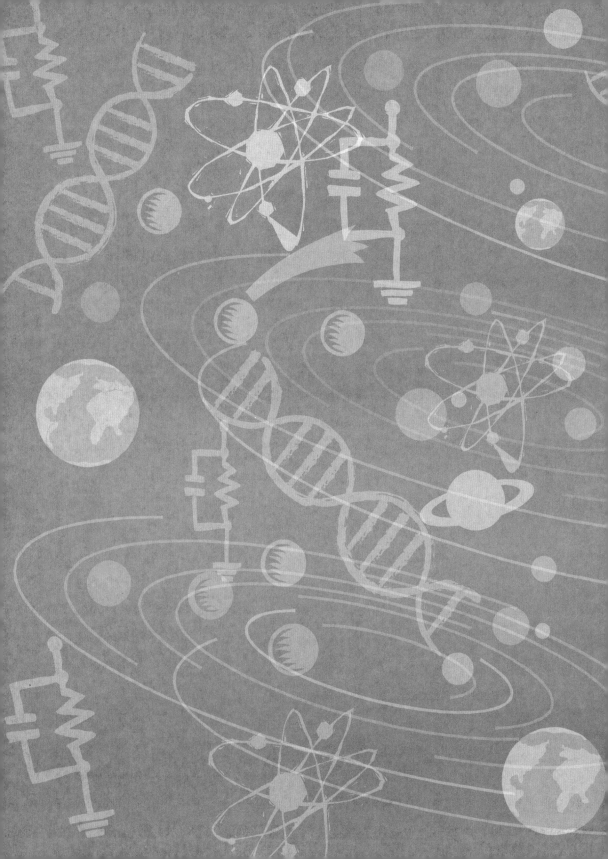